W9-BEE-222

A DORLING KINDERSLEY BOOK
Conceived, edited, and designed by DK Direct Limited

Note to parents

What's Inside? Sea Creatures is designed to help young children understand the magical world of life under the sea. It shows where to find a starfish's mouth, how a barnacle opens its shell, and where an octopus keeps its ink. It is a book for you and your child to read and talk about together, and to enjoy.

Editor Hilary Hockman
Designer John Strange
Typographic Designer Nigel Coath
U.S. Editor Laaren Brown

Illustrators Stuart Lafford/Linden Artists, Barry Robson/Linden Artists, Steve Weston/Linden Artists
Written by Alexandra Parsons
Consultant Theresa Greenaway
Design Director Ed Day
Editorial Director Jonathan Reed

Picture Credits Francisco Futil/Bruce Coleman Ltd. (pp. 12-13), Allan Power/Bruce Coleman Ltd. (p. 8), Bill Wood/Bruce Coleman Ltd. (pp. 12-13). Additional photography by Dave King.

First American Edition, 1993

10 9 8 7 6 5 4 3 2 1

Published in the United States by
Dorling Kindersley, Inc., 232 Madison Avenue
New York, New York 10016

Library of Congress Cataloging-in-Publication Data
Sea creatures. – 1st American ed.
p. cm. – (What's inside?)
Summary: Explores the habitats, behavior, and anatomy of such sea creatures as the barnacle, starfish, and shark.
ISBN 1-56458-221-3
1. Marine fauna – Anatomy – Juvenile literature.
[1. Marine animals.] I. Series.
QL122.2.S38 1993
591.92 — dc20   92-54274 CIP AC

Printed in Italy

WHAT'S INSIDE?
SEA CREATURES

DK

DORLING KINDERSLEY
LONDON • NEW YORK • STUTTGART

SHARK

The shark is a powerful swimming and hunting machine with huge gaping jaws and teeth as sharp as daggers. It swims with a smooth, speedy action, and it can sniff out prey for miles around. There are hundreds of different kinds of sharks, but don't worry – not many of them are a danger to swimmers. The longest is the whale shark, 39 feet long. The smallest is the pygmy – only about 8 inches in length.

The top half of the tail is like a giant, dangerous whip.

Sharks don't have bones. Their skeletons are made of cartilage, a tough but bendy material.

This is a thresher shark. They grow to about 16 feet long, and half of that is tail!

Sharks don't have scales on their skin. They have denticles, which are like little tooth-shaped plates. The denticles are very sharp.

Not surprisingly, sharks have an endless supply of teeth. If a tooth gets worn out or broken, another one moves forward to take its place.

Sharks can hunt out prey even when they can't see it. They can "smell" and "taste" what's swimming around in the water as it passes through their nostrils and mouth.

A heavy shark would sink to the bottom of the ocean if it didn't have a big liver full of oil. The oil is lighter than water, and it acts as an internal float to help the shark swim.

Thresher sharks have five gill slits on each side.

Powerful jaw muscles help the shark snap down on its prey.

The shark's brain is quite big ... for a fish! Sharks are smarter than the average fish, and in captivity they can even learn tricks.

STARFISH

What a strange animal the starfish is! It lives in the sea, but cannot swim. It has five arms and hundreds of feet. It has a stomach that can turn inside out, and it has absolutely no brains at all. Starfish creep around on rocks and along the ocean floor, and they can even crawl up strands of seaweed.

Each foot is a tiny tube with a sucker on the end. The starfish uses its feet to hold on to rocks and to pull open the shells of its prey.

The starfish has an unusual approach to mealtimes. It takes its stomach to the food instead of taking the food to its stomach! First it opens the shell of its victim just a crack. Then the starfish turns its own stomach inside-out through its mouth and pushes its stomach into the opened shell.

And now for something even stranger ... if a starfish loses an arm, it can grow another one within a week or two.

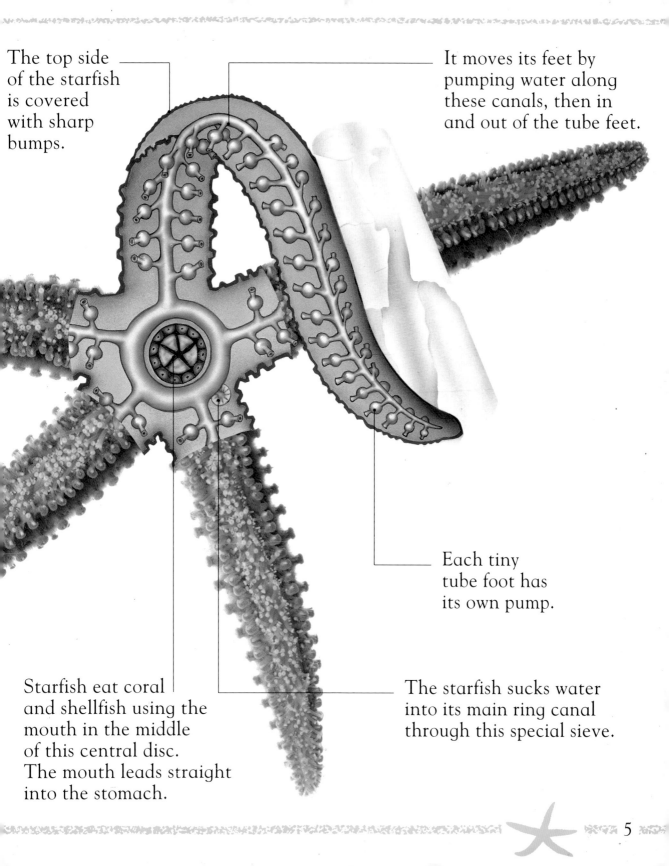

The top side of the starfish is covered with sharp bumps.

It moves its feet by pumping water along these canals, then in and out of the tube feet.

Each tiny tube foot has its own pump.

Starfish eat coral and shellfish using the mouth in the middle of this central disc. The mouth leads straight into the stomach.

The starfish sucks water into its main ring canal through this special sieve.

BARNACLE

These tiny shellfish live in groups on rocks, on shipwrecks, or on the shells of bigger shellfish. Some, called goose barnacles, have stalks and live on floating things. Acorn barnacles, another kind, don't have stalks. They cover the rocks at the seashore and make it very painful to walk barefoot. Barnacles stick themselves down with a special cement. If you've ever tried to scrape barnacles off something, you know just how strong that cement can be!

There's not much to see on the outside. This is a cluster of goose barnacles. Their shells are divided into five sections. The sections open when the barnacle is hungry.

Baby barnacles float around in the sea until it is time to settle down and cement themselves to a rock for the rest of their lives.

Barnacles often make themselves at home on the bottoms of boats. They have to be scraped off because their weight slows the boat down.

The food goes in here, then travels down to the stomach. Waste comes out at the end of the stomach tube.

These feathery feet are called cirri. The barnacle pushes them out through the openings in its shell and waves them around to catch scraps of food floating in the water.

This muscle opens and closes the shell.

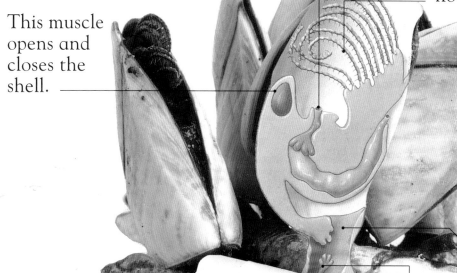

Here is the stalk. The barnacle can pull the stalk inside its shell or push it out.

This is the gland that makes the cement that glues the barnacle to its rock.

MORAY EEL

Eels are fish, but they look more like snakes. They are long and wriggly, and they glide through the sea like giant ribbons. This fearsome-looking tropical moray eel lives in the Pacific Ocean. It spends its days hidden among the rocks with just its hungry head poking out.

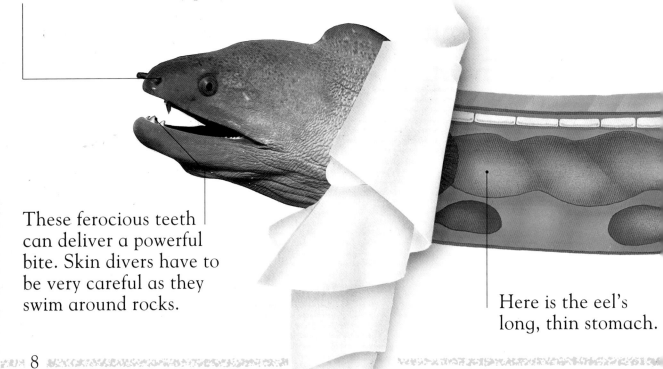

Water passes through these nostrils, so the eel can "smell" the water for nearby prey.

These ferocious teeth can deliver a powerful bite. Skin divers have to be very careful as they swim around rocks.

Here is the eel's long, thin stomach.

Long ago, sailors told terrible tales of great writhing sea monsters. Now we think that these "sea monsters" were nothing more than large eels.

A moray eel can grow up to 9 feet long. That's almost the length of a family car!

Here's the eel's long, strong tail.

Waste matter comes out here, about half-way along.

The eel belongs to the huge family of bony fish. But the eel, of course, has more bones than most in its long, long backbone.

LOBSTER

Shellfish, like this lobster, belong to a family of animals called crustaceans. The lobster's closest relations are crabs, crayfish, and shrimps. They all have a hard outer covering of shell, like a suit of armor, and a soft body inside.

When the lobster grows, it sheds its shell. Its new, bigger shell is soft, so the lobster has to hide away for about three days until it hardens.

The lobster has a very simple blood supply system. The heart keeps its blood moving.

This powerful muscle moves the lobster's springy tail.

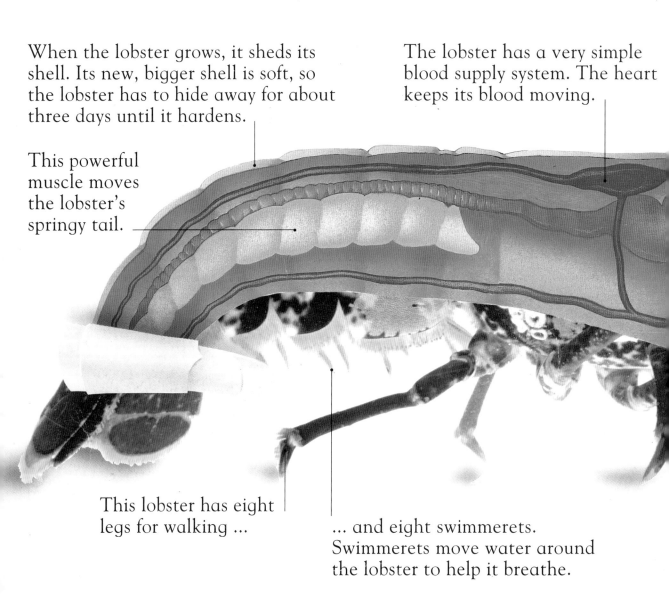

This lobster has eight legs for walking ...

... and eight swimmerets. Swimmerets move water around the lobster to help it breathe.

Spiny lobsters that live in tropical seas go on a long journey every year, marching along the ocean bed in long lines. It's thought they do this to get away from colder winter water.

Watch out! The lobster uses its heavy front claws to attack and protect itself from enemies.

The brain is just behind the eye.

The stomach is right here, where you might expect its brain to be!

Here's the lobster's mouth.

The sharp edges of the claws help the lobster tear its food to pieces.

CORAL

This beautiful underwater garden is not made of weeds and rocks, but of tiny sea creatures. These hard coral polyps are very simple animals with a stony skeleton on the outside and a soft little body like a sack inside. They grow in warm, sunlit, shallow seas.

Red coral is used to make coral jewelry. Coral grows at the same rate as fingernails, so you can imagine how long this necklace took to grow!

By day the polyps stay inside their stony homes, and the reef looks like lumps of lifeless rock. But at night the polyps shoot out their tentacles to feed, and the reef comes magically to life.

Corals come in wonderful shapes – with wonderful names like "dead man's fingers," "brain coral," "staghorn coral," and "fan coral."

Coral polyps are crowned with a ring of tentacles, which they wave around to catch the food wafting by. They eat fish eggs and incredibly tiny sea creatures. Some corals have stinging tentacles that can kill or knock out their prey.

The stomach is lined with folds of soft flesh.

The mouth is in the middle.

At the bottom of the polyp is a cup of stony skeleton that anchors it to its neighbors. When this polyp dies, a new polyp can grow on top, so the old skeleton becomes a building block in the growth of a coral reef.

OCTOPUS

The octopus, like its relations the squid and the cuttlefish, looks as if it's all head and arms. But the big bulge behind the head is its body. The octopus moves along backward by sucking water into its body and squirting it out. Every octopus has eight long, strong arms, or tentacles. It can change color to match its surroundings or when it's angry or excited.

The octopus has a very clever trick to confuse its enemies. It can squirt inky water out of its siphon hole and disappear in a big black cloud.

The better to see you with! An octopus has very good eyesight.

The arms of an ordinary octopus can be up to 8 feet long. It uses them for walking as well as for catching crabs, which are its favorite food.

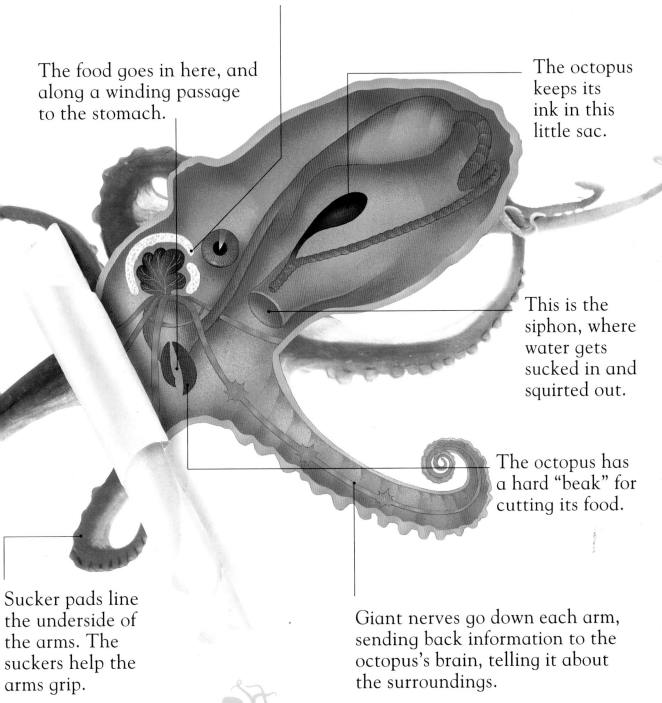

The brain of the octopus is protected by a skull made of cartilage.

The food goes in here, and along a winding passage to the stomach.

The octopus keeps its ink in this little sac.

This is the siphon, where water gets sucked in and squirted out.

The octopus has a hard "beak" for cutting its food.

Sucker pads line the underside of the arms. The suckers help the arms grip.

Giant nerves go down each arm, sending back information to the octopus's brain, telling it about the surroundings.

BLOWFISH

When all is going well for a blowfish, it looks just like a
fattish fish with big eyes. But an angry or frightened blowfish is
quite a sight! It gulps in water and blows itself up like a huge
balloon. This blowfish looks really scary when it's puffed up
because its long scales stand up like the spines of a porcupine.

This blowfish has puffed
itself up to frighten off
an enemy. Another fish
would have trouble
swallowing it now!

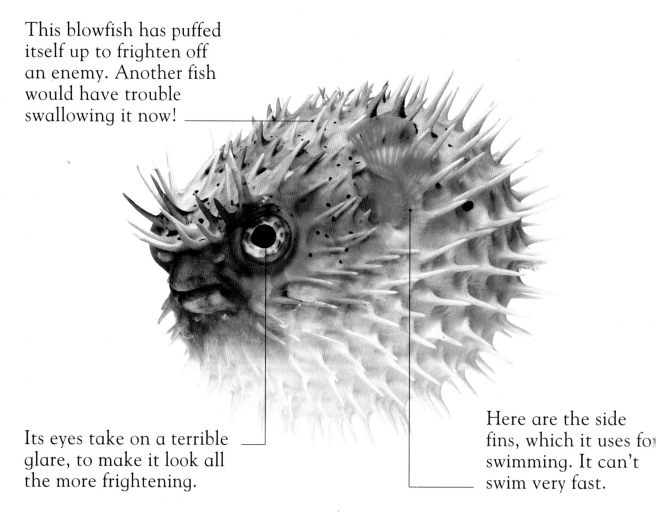

Its eyes take on a terrible
glare, to make it look all
the more frightening.

Here are the side
fins, which it uses for
swimming. It can't
swim very fast.

In Japan, certain blowfish, called *fugu*, are a great delicacy. Special chefs have to train for years, learning to cut out the poisonous bits. They make the fish safe to eat, but leave just the right touch of mouth-tingling poison.

Like most fish with a bony skeleton, the blowfish has a little bag of gas inside it called a swim bladder. This keeps the fish from sinking to the bottom of the sea.

The blowfish uses its hard "beak" to crush small shellfish and other tiny sea animals for food.

To blow up, the blowfish sucks water into its stretchy stomach.

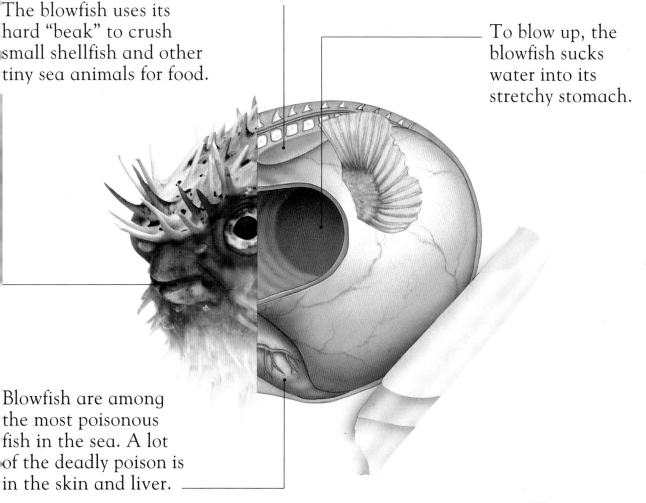

Blowfish are among the most poisonous fish in the sea. A lot of the deadly poison is in the skin and liver.